W9-BLP-123

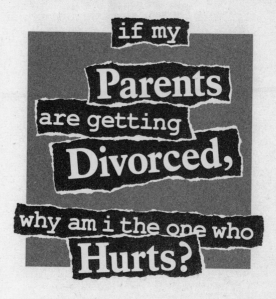

if my Parents are getting Divorced, why am i the one who Hurts?

Jeenie Gordon

ZondervanPublishingHouse
Grand Rapids, Michigan

A Division of HarperCollins*Publishers*

If My Parents Are Getting Divorced, Why Am I the One Who Hurts?
Copyright © 1993 by Jeenie Gordon

Requests for information should be addressed to:
Zondervan Publishing House
Grand Rapids, Michigan 49530

ISBN 0-310-59311-5

All Scripture quotations, unless otherwise noted, are taken from the
HOLY BIBLE: NEW INTERNATIONAL VERSION®. Copyright ©
1973, 1978, 1984 by International Bible Society. Used by permission of
Zondervan Publishing House. All rights reserved.

All rights reserved. No part of this publication may be reproduced,
stored in a retrieval system, or transmitted in any form or by any
means—electronic, mechanical, photocopy, recording, or any other—
except for brief quotations in printed reviews, without the prior
permission of the publisher.

Edited by Jan Ortiz
Cover design by Jerry Fahselt

Printed in the United States of America

93 94 95 96 97 / DH / 10 9 8 7 6 5 4 3 2 1

To my daughter, brother, and sister

Kathi Lundstrom
Ben West
Ruby White

Children of divorce
who have become healthy survivors

Contents

Foreword

When a family system crumbles as a result of divorce, teenagers quickly discover that they are both orphans and victims of that life-shattering experience. The family that nurtured them disappears overnight, and they are left to struggle with their feelings of abandonment, anger, fear, and pain. As a pioneer in the field of divorce recovery, I have listened to twenty years worth of frustration and feelings expressed by teenagers who have fallen victim to living out a decision their parents have made.

My friend Jeenie Gordon has written a concise and caring book that will bring hope back into the life of any teenager struggling with the whiplash of divorce. Her book is honest and practical, and it deals with all the basic issues and struggles teenagers go through when divorce strikes their family. It is a book parents can give to their teenagers and a book teenagers can use and pass on to their friends. It provides no easy answers, for there are none, but it speaks to the pain divorce causes and offers a light at the end of the tunnel for all who read it.

Jim Smoke
Director
The Center for Divorce Recovery
Tempe, Arizona

Preface

"Why don't you write a book for teenagers whose parents have divorced? We desperately need one." This was the advice I heard numerous times as I conducted seminars for pastors and youth pastors.

I searched the bookstores. Little to nothing has been written to adolescents who are experiencing the gut-wrenching pain of their parents' separation or divorce. Therefore, after completing a book for adults, *Cementing the Torn Strands: Rebuilding Your Life After Divorce* (Fleming H. Revell), I began this book.

All names of persons from my counseling practice whose stories are shared have been changed, as have their situations, in order to protect their privacy.

Letters from readers are always appreciated. I am also available for speaking engagements and may be contacted at the following address:

New Hope Counseling
908 South Village Oaks Drive
Suite 250
Covina, CA 91724
818-967-6421

Acknowledgments

With gratefulness, I thank my editor, David Lambert, for his wise input and editorial direction. My appreciation extends as well to the support staff at Zondervan.

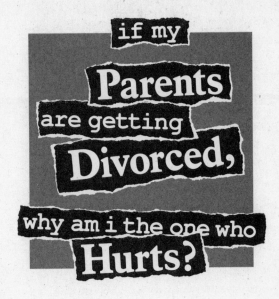

if my **Parents** are getting **Divorced,** why am i the one who **Hurts?**

Introduction

This book is about hope.

"Excuse me," you mutter. "Hope?"

That's right, hope. But to get to hope we must first look at some circumstances that surround divorce.

- When parents break up, the future looks bleak—even nonexistent. A lot of changes take place. Life is not very pretty.
- Sometimes you're told with whom you will live. Other times you are expected to make an almost impossible choice between your mother and your father.
- Often the family home is sold. Most of the time the part of the family that stays together is squeezed into a much smaller, less comfortable place.
- Separation and divorce usually play havoc with the wallet. Current statistics cite that a woman's income *drops* 73 percent when a divorce takes place. Studies have proven that divorced or separated women, along with their children, have been added in large numbers to the lower-class population of our society. They have become the new poor.

Now, I admit all this doesn't look very hopeful.

But hang with me. In order to heal, you must have hope. I've counseled over eight thousand teenagers, many from divorced homes, and I have listened to their painful stories. Because of what I have learned from these teens, I want to walk you through the process of healing. I want to help you acknowledge and name your feelings, understand them, and work through them. My desire is that you come through the gut-wrenching experience of divorce as an emotionally strong and healthy person.

Learning to cope in a healthy way is important, and my desire is to guide you. We will look at the destructive things you tell yourself and explore ways in which to change. I'll show you how to make a plan for your life—how to be self-directed and productive. As the chapters unfold, you'll learn how to deal more effectively with your parents and keep them on your side. We'll talk about how to be honest with yourself and others so you can be free.

I have seen many a teen recover from their parents' divorce.

That's my desire for you.

1

How Can I Survive?

"Survive? Impossible!" Allison screamed. "I'm just hanging on by my fingernails now, and one by one they're breaking. Frankly, I don't even want to live. Life's just not worth it. I can't stand this."

Even though her green eyes were snapping with anger, I could see the intense hurt they held.

"It really does seem like this is the end, doesn't it, Allison?" I said. "Life seems over. Done with. You wonder, 'What's the use?'

"There's good news, though. There's *hope*—and *healing*. It doesn't happen overnight. It's a process. There are steps you'll have to take, but eventually you will be whole."

The Steps of Healing

Elizabeth Kübler-Ross came up with a wonderful idea of how we get better. She's a psychologist who separated the healing process into stages. For our purposes, we will call these stages, *steps*.

When tragedy first strikes, we are forced onto the first step—instant *denial*. We hurt so badly that we can't face the possibility that the tragedy might be true. So, we deny it. In denial, we feel as though we're numb. We are. Nature is anesthetizing us from the intensity of the pain.

We say things like, "I can't believe this is happening." Or, "This can't be real." Or, "When I wake up, I'll realize this is all just a bad dream—a nightmare. It'll be okay."

But when we awake, it's still there. And it continues to hurt until we think we can't stand it anymore. Even though you really hurt, don't deny denial. Allow yourself to deny. It's okay. It's a very important step in the healing process. Someday, after you have healed, you will be able to accept the reality of your parents' divorce, even if, at first, you deny.

Another step of healing is *anger*. Not the mild, ticked-off kind. No. This anger is rage. Fury.

Adolescents, especially males, are often more in touch with their anger than with any other emotion. They explode. They are furious. They often go on a rampage. "I don't deserve this!" they holler. "It's not fair. God, how could you do this to me?" All the while they flail their way through the world feeling absolutely helpless and hopeless.

Jeff came to my office to vent his anger. I sat quietly while he screamed, swore, slung his arms, shouted, and slapped the desk. Then the tears came. Silently he cried.

"Jeff," I said tenderly, "we need to find the source

of your fury. Tell me why you're so angry. What are your other feelings?"

"It just hurts so much. I feel abandoned, left, forsaken, alone, scared."

One by one, we began to talk through his feelings, and he could see his outrage was the result of these underlying emotions. There was a root to his rage. Discovering the basis for his rage helped Jeff begin to dissipate it.

As the example of Jeff illustrates, a good way to deal with anger is to think, "What am I *really* feeling?" Then, begin to name those feelings—"left out, afraid, dumped, alone . . ." The anger is the outward expression of what's happening on the inside. Acknowledge the internal feelings. Admit them. Another step on the ladder of grief has been traversed.

Bargaining is yet another step in the healing process. We bargain by saying, "If only I had . . ." or, "Why didn't I . . ." or, "I wish I had . . ." Teens hold a mythical belief that they could have *done* something about their parents' divorce—stopped it or even prevented it from happening.

Leaning forward, I tried to hear what Jeff was saying. Softly he mumbled (probably more to himself than to me), "I should've studied more. I didn't care that much about my grades. And if I would have cleaned my room and picked up the mess, all this wouldn't have happened."

Not so.

Some people go beyond bargaining with themselves and begin to bargain with God. "Listen, God, I promise you I'll go to church every Sunday, even if I'm half dead. Don't let this divorce happen." Or, "I won't have sex at all before I'm married. In fact, I'll not even *think* about it. Just please, please make it okay with my parents."

Bargaining is a *normal* process. Allow yourself to go through this part of grief. Give yourself some slack.

Eventually, though, we learn that the problem with bargaining is that it doesn't work. Nothing changes.

When we learn that bargaining doesn't stop the divorce, we hit *deep depression*. Depression is that stage of grief where you feel as though you are being sucked into a huge black hole. From the darkness, everything looks bleak. You aren't sleeping well. You don't notice if the sun is shining—nor do you care. In fact, you aren't concerned about much of anything. School and grades are last on the list. Why try? Nothing matters.

It is *vital* that you talk to someone when depression hits. Seek out a person who will listen—a friend, coach, teacher, neighbor, counselor, family member (sibling, aunt, uncle, grandparent). Tell them how you feel. Don't be ashamed to let the tears come. Tears and talk aid healing.

The last step toward the resolution of grief is *acceptance*. It's that point at which the enormous pain is gone. We may still have moments of hurt, but the hurt does not *rule* our lives. We've accepted the divorce. For the most part, it's all right and we're okay.

An organization for teens called Step II adds another step to the stages of Kübler-Ross—*hope*. Hope is vital to recovery from the grief that divorce brings. Hope helps us hang on. It suggests that life will be good again, for someday the pain will be gone and we will, once more, feel comfortable. Hope gives us courage.

I choose to put these stages into steps because we experience them over and over in varying degrees and sequences. There is no specific order. We continually move among these stages throughout the healing process.

> *hope*
> *acceptance*
> *depression*
> *bargaining*
> *anger*
> *denial*

We can experience all of these emotions in only a matter of five minutes. Or we may spend weeks or months in one or two of the stages while we seem to breeze through the rest. However, it is rare that healing takes place rapidly. We constantly go back and forth.

During that visit, Jeff related, "My dad said,

'Could you come in here a minute? Your mom and I want to talk to you kids about a serious matter.' We all gathered around. Then he said, 'We have decided to get a divorce.'

"Dad could have pulled a gun on me and I wouldn't have been any more surprised," Jeff told me.

"This just can't be true," he continued (*denial*). "I don't want to live anymore. It hurts too much (*depression*). If only I'd obeyed my parents, they'd still be together (*bargaining*). I could kill 'em. It's so unfair (*anger*). Maybe we'll all be better off" (*acceptance and hope*).

Jeff expressed all of these emotional stages in a few short sentences in a minimal period of time. However, it will take much longer to completely work through the stages. But when permanent healing begins to occur, we find ourselves in the various steps for *shorter* periods of time. A longer length of time begins to elapse *between* stages as well.

For instance, we get depressed, but it doesn't last too long. And a longer time period passes before we are depressed again.

Feeling the Pain

It's vital that we allow ourselves to intensely *feel* the pain. The American tendency is to stuff it down. Try to get rid of it. Avoid it.

However, *walking* through the trauma is essential. We much prefer to *run* like crazy—to get it over with. But working through the steps of healing takes time. When we give ourselves permission to take all the time we need, we will eventually come out emotionally healthy.

Thinking It Over

1. In looking at the steps of healing, list how each is impacting you.

   Denial:

   Anger:

   Bargaining:

   Depression:

   Acceptance:

   Hope:

2. Have you experienced all of these steps? Which ones are missing? Are you "stuck" in one of them?

2

That Normal Feeling

"Amy, I haven't seen you in years! How are you?" I exclaimed as she walked into my office.

"Good. Really good," she replied.

"What are you doing now?"

With a glint in her eye, and a smile that rippled across her freckled face, she said, "I'm at the university. Next year I'll be a senior. Can't believe it."

"Wonderful!" I said.

Old Normal

Memories flooded back. It seemed that hundreds of pictures flitted across the screen of my mind.

When I had first met Amy, it was to register her for high school. She was a bouncy, cute, vibrant, and happy junior higher. Her goals were high, and she insisted on honors courses. Amy knew what she wanted and she was going for it—full force. She appeared to feel good about herself and exuded excitement and the joy of being alive.

Most of the time, we live life as though we are in

a groove. Like a rope that is held by the pulley's groove, we move through our day-to-day lives without having to do a lot of thinking or planning. We're comfortable. Normal.

We get up, shower, brush our teeth, comb our hair, eat breakfast, go to school, return home, study, kick back—then, do it all over again the next day. A lot of life is rather uneventful—boring, even. We glide through our days without major interruptions.

Actually, life like this is rather nice. Routines are good. We feel normal.

Abnormal

"Remember when my parents split up in my freshman year?" Amy said. "It seemed I was always crying in your office. I was so devastated. I felt like I'd never smile again. Life was over."

I sure did remember. This once vibrant girl had seemed to disintegrate before my eyes.

"Life is just not worth living," she had sobbed. "Nothing matters anymore. I don't feel like me. It's—like weird. I hate being like this."

When trauma hits, we're knocked out of the groove. Life has no boundaries. We feel uncomfortable, strange, weird, abnormal. All during the healing process (which could be months or even years), we do not feel like our usual selves. We begin to think that we'll never feel normal again.

Yet, strange as it seems, these abnormal feelings

are actually *normal* based on the blow we've received. Shock spins us into an uncomfortable and unreal state of feeling.

It's okay to feel *abnormal*, especially the first few months after your parents' divorce. During the time of healing, allow yourself to feel peculiar. Don't deny the feelings. Don't pretend they don't exist.

New Normal

"The thing that probably impacted me the most," Amy added, "was when you told me about the *new normal*. It made me feel okay about the divorce."

Eventually you will work through your pain and someday establish a new normal. You'll feel okay again. You'll feel comfortable and satisfied. In the new normal, parents will still be divorced. But you will have gained enough growth and insight to be okay with it. You've accepted it.

The new normal in Amy's case was a separate and different relationship with each parent. You can also experience a new relationship with each of your parents. Often, as with Amy, it is better than before. If you muster up enough courage to be honest in a caring and kind way, the connection with your parents will be even more loving and real. Sometimes after a divorce, there is more opportunity to see each parent as a *person*, who can become a valued friend.

"Even though I'm living with Mom," Amy said,

"I have a new relationship with Dad. He's become my pal and confidant. Tuesday night is our 'date' night. We go out to dinner and talk and talk and talk. No way would I have dreamed that our relationship could be this good. We've finally become father and daughter."

Amy's newfound friendship with her dad came about because she was willing to make him a part of her life. She was honest about her feelings and did not deny the pain. She chose to "bury the hatchet," and to forgive.

A New Life

Establishing a new normal isn't always easy. The first step is to admit your pain—call a spade a spade. Quit denying. Second, confront the issues with the parent by being truthful and kind. Third, begin a forgiveness process (more on this subject later). Last, be willing to have a friendship—even if it means making the first move.

After establishing a new normal, it would seem strange to go back to your old normal (before the painful event). That part of your life is gone forever. It's been replaced.

Amy said, "When you first explained this concept to me, I never dreamed it could be true, but it is. I have a new life now. It's great, and I feel good again. When I look back on the painful times, it hardly seems real. There really *is* a new normal. And, I'm there."

*   *   *

> When we are willing to do our part—
>   Admit our pain
>   Confront in love
>   Forgive
>   Allow friendship—
> Healing will come.

Thinking It Over

1. **"Old" Normal**
   Write a few sentences about your lifestyle
   before the separation of your parents.

2. **Abnormal**
   Name some of your feelings (abandonment,
   fear, loneliness, anger, etc.)

   I feel

   I feel

   I feel

   I feel

   I feel

3. **"New" Normal**
   Write down several *goals* for your new life.

   a.

   b.

   c.

3

Coping with This Mess

Jason charged into my office, slammed the door, and plopped himself into the nearest chair. "I can't stand this any more!" he yelled, his voice shaking.

He pounded his fist on my desk. His eyes blazed with anger and bitter tears. Struggling to quiet himself, he tipped back the chair and said, "You know, Mrs. Gordon, I was going home to blow out my brains. But first, I just had to come to talk."

Quietly, I waited while he cried.

Then we talked—for two hours.

Destructive Coping

We *must* cope. In fact, we *always* cope. There are two ways of coping—destructive coping and constructive coping.

Destructive coping behaviors include such things as attempting suicide, taking drugs, drinking, and sexual involvement—all things that will bring great harm.

Jason's idea of coping was to kill himself. He felt that by committing suicide his problem would be "over." Suicide never works out that neatly, though. Jason's killing himself would not solve the underlying problem. And Jason would not be "gone" either. The memory of him would live on. His family and friends would experience enormous pain for years because of his foolish choice.

As a high-school counselor, rarely has a year passed that I have not looked into a white casket that has held the body of an adolescent who has taken his or her own life. The death mask is imprinted on a face that is far too young. Too soon life has ended because she or he decided to cope with problems in a *destructive* way. Parents and family are nearly destroyed because a precious teen has been wrenched from his or her place in life. I've watched the unchecked tears and listened to the audible weeping of their classmates.

Suicide *never* resolves a painful situation. It creates anguish.

During the last four months of this school year three students from the school where I work died in automobile accidents. Drugs and alcohol were involved in all three tragedies. It happens nearly every year.

Four senior boys spent Saturday morning in the park smoking marijuana and doing a variety of drugs. By midafternoon, they decided to go for a ride. Piling into a car, they raced through town at high speeds, crossed a divided highway into oncoming traffic, and met their fate. Their bodies were hurled from the automobile. Two lay dead. One was hospitalized for months and has never regained the ability to think rationally.

In an unchaperoned party where alcohol flowed, a group of boys challenged two girls to a drag race. At 2:00 A.M. they floorboarded their engines. The deafening sound of a car crashing into a brick wall was heard a half mile away. The girl who was driving survived. But she spent weeks in the hospital to heal physically, then months in a psychiatric ward. Her best friend was buried—in her prom dress.

Alcohol and drugs remove inhibitions and greatly blur the ability to make rational choices. Sometimes a teen indulges in alcohol or drugs to dull emotional pain, but often it is done with friends just to have a good time. Tragedy is the result.

Sexual activity is another destructive way to cope with pain. During the years that I have been a counselor, I've seen scores of young pregnant girls. Very often it's the girl's first sexual encounter. Some of these girls choose to keep their babies, and their adolescent years end abruptly. School, ball games, dates, and fun get put on the back burner. Motherhood takes over—completely. Others decide abortion is the best option. Then they try to cope with the aftermath of depression and guilt.

Destructive coping is a choice. It seems easy, but it doesn't work. It only compounds the pain. No one needs to choose paths that will bring further trauma into his or her life. Drugs, sex, alcohol, and suicide don't make the pain go away. They just dull the pain—for a while. Then it's all back again. Nothing is resolved.

When the "throw-it-all-away" urge overwhelms you and you want to give in to destructive coping, find an adult friend. Talk it out.

Jason hit my office before he decided to pull the trigger. He's so glad he did!

Here are some ways in which you can change the destructive path and cope in healthy ways.

Constructive Coping

Constructive coping provides eventual solutions and healing.

Crying is one positive way in which to deal with pain. Never be ashamed of tears. Let them flow. Cry alone as well as with someone you can trust. Tears wash away some of the hurt and bring refreshment and healing. People who bottle up their tears become emotionally unhealthy.

In *Cementing the Torn Strands*, I tell the story of my dog, Lady. She was my buddy, my constant companion whom I adored. But one day I peered more closely into her soft brown eyes and realized she was very ill. My heart jumped. I thought, *My dog's dying.*

Tenderly I laid her in my car. Tears came in torrents as I gently stroked her limp body on the seat next to me. As I drove, I made the painful decision that if it were serious, I would put her to sleep.

"Her kidneys have failed," stated the doctor. "I can hospitalize her and operate, but there's not much hope. Perhaps she could live a few more days. What do you want to do?"

"I've made my decision," I said. "I want you to put her to sleep while I'm here with her." The tears were cascading from my eyes, plummeting down my face. I could hardly see.

The doctor prepared the serum. I patted her lovingly while he injected her. In a few moments, her breathing stopped. Quietly he said, "She's gone. I'll leave you alone with her for a bit."

As my tears splashed on her lifeless form, I gently slid my fingers through her gray fur and took off her collar and name tag. "God," I cried, "Thank you for the years I've had Lady. She has been such a precious little pal to me—a special gift from you." The vet carried her out.

For two days I cried enormous tears. It was almost as though I were "throwing up" the pain inside—it came spurting out.

Previously in my life's traumas (the divorce of my parents, my mother's early death, and my own divorce), I'd always been the one who "held up well." I let my pain seep out, rather than gush. In fact, I had always been rather disgusted with people who became hysterical in their pain.

When Lady died, however, I learned a valuable lesson. My willingness to be overwrought and to let the pain come swirling out made me feel better.

When we hold in the pain or merely let it seep out over time, our healing process is hindered and lengthened. People from cultures where pain is expressed with loud crying, beating of chests, and wailing make use of a healthy emotional outlet. They are able to heal more quickly because they really "get into" their pain. Seepage is unhealthy. Let the pain erupt.

I admire Jason. He was a virile eighteen-year-old male who was not ashamed nor afraid to let the tears flow—tears that brought healing.

Another healthy coping strategy is talking. Find an adult who will not give advice or judge, but who will just listen. As we talk, we gain insight. Talking allows us to understand our feelings to a greater degree. Often a route emerges, guiding us toward the right direction. Rather than killing himself, Jason let out his pain and anger through tears and talking. He came often.

Finding a strategy to cope with anger can be difficult. Males often hit things and sometimes will put a fist through a wall. I've seen a number of hands and fingers broken in this way. It is more healthy to *talk* out your anger with a friend. Identify the *underlying* feelings that bring about the rage.

Ask yourself: "What are my feelings? Do I feel despairing? Scared? Hopeless? Desolate? Forsaken?

Downcast? Isolated? Despondent? Powerless? Defenseless? Humiliated? Abandoned? Helpless? Alone? Name your feelings. Admit them. Then, give yourself permission to feel what you feel. This is the way you deal with the *root* of the anger. Someday the feelings will fade.

*   *   *

"Want to see my baby girl?" Jason asked as he bounded into my office three years later. Slinging his leg over the arm of the chair, he gently picked up an adorable two-year-old and placed her on his knee. A smile was splashed all over this proud father's face. His tiny, blue-eyed, blond daughter giggled.

"You know, I'm married, and this is my pride and joy. Isn't she precious? I'm an electrician apprentice and doing really good on my job. Life is super."

He could have been dead, I thought, *and missed all this.*

"Jason," I responded, "I'm so very proud of you. I've always believed in you."

*   *   *

Jason's constructive method of coping has given him a good life. *Look for an adult who will befriend you.* It could be a teacher, youth pastor, counselor, neighbor, employer, relative, or coach. They're out there. Don't give up until you find one. Then, be honest and express your pain. Talk, talk, talk.

Make a decision to cope constructively and go for it. You're worth it!

Thinking It Over

Coping is tough, but it must be done.
1. In what ways are you choosing to cope *destructively*?

    a.

    b.

    c.

    d.

    e.

2. How are you coping in a *constructive* way?

    a.

    b.

    c.

    d.

    e.

3. Think through two ideas of how you can cope in a healthy way.

    a.

    b.

4

Stuff I Tell Myself

Ever talk to yourself—or answer? We do it constantly. Sometimes out loud, but more often it's just in our minds.

When we converse, we speak about two hundred to three hundred words a minute. However, when we talk to ourselves, it's about *thirteen hundred words* a minute. We tell ourselves far more than does anyone else. We hear far more from ourselves than from anyone else. Our brain whirls—seemingly never stopping.

Most of our problems come because we're telling ourselves a lot of nonsense. Unfortunately, it's easy to begin to believe our nonsense and act accordingly. Then, in time, what was never really true becomes true.

Very likely you've told yourself some of these things:

- "With my parents splitting up, life's over."
- "There's just no way out."
- "I'm never going to survive this."
- "No one understands—or cares—how I feel."

● "I can just dump all my dreams for my future."

These statements are negative self-talk. They bring about discouragement, depression, hopelessness, and a give-up attitude.

Shelley

"I'm here to see Shelley," I told the receptionist at the psychiatric hospital.

"Uh, huh. Okay," mumbled the lady. Looking over the visitor clipboard, she commented, "Name's not here." Clumsily covering an afternoon yawn, she continued, "You can't come in."

"I spoke to the psychiatrist yesterday and received clearance," I said. "He said I'd be allowed in since I'm Shelley's high-school counselor, and also a marriage, family, and child therapist in private practice. I'd appreciate your checking with Dr. Burns."

Nonchalantly pushing the intercom number, she said, "Dr. Burns, a lady wants to see Shelley. The name is Gordon."

Then, with a wordless wave of the hand, she sent me into the locked ward.

"Shelley to the visitor's room," came the message over the loud speaker.

She came bouncing through the double doors with a wide smile painted across her face, grabbed me in a tight hug, and said, "You really came."

As I listened to her story, I was shocked to see

bloody red gashes covering her wrists. Looking into her sky-blue eyes, I saw a precious teen with a model's figure, shiny black hair resting on her shoulders, and a smile that could melt a December snow. *How could she have done this!* I thought. *She has so much going for her. What a dear, desperate girl.*

Over the next few years, Shelley kept in touch. But even with all the help she received, she was unable to come to grips with her parents' divorce. Her grades plummeted, she wound up in an alternative high school program, yet she never graduated.

Like Shelley, we could sincerely believe that horrible things are the result of a life trauma.

However, it's not true!

The A, B, Cs

Dr. Ellis, a psychologist, formulated what he calls the A, B, C Theory.

A represents the *activating event* (parents' separation and divorce).

B stands for the *belief* we have about the event.

C stands for the *consequences.* Everyone "knows" that *bad* events bring *awful* consequences.

The Big B

Which one of the three letters is the most important when we're trying to cope? Is it A—the activating event? B—our belief about the event? Or C—the consequences of the event? You guessed it—it's B!

B stands for the *belief* we have about a situation. The *belief* is what determines the consequences, not the event. If we *believe* life is over and that nothing good will ever come along, that's exactly what will happen.

Activating Event	Negative Belief	Bad Consequences
Divorce	Life's ended for me.	Depression Giving up

However, the good news is that we can *change* our *belief* about the separation or divorce.

Activating Event	Positive Belief	Good Consequences
Divorce	It's bad, but I'm a survivor. I'll get through this and be okay.	Working through the steps of healing and becoming emotionally healthy.

Sometimes we don't have control over what happens to us in life, but we have a choice as to how we *respond* to it. Shelley is still aimless. She's unwilling to change her belief about the divorce. Jason, too, wanted to kill himself but chose to take the positive road. Life for him is good.

Choose well, for your reaction will determine the quality of the rest of your life.

Thinking It Over

Divorce

1. What *negative* things do I believe about it?

   a.

   b.

   c.

   d.

2. What *negative consequences* may happen because of my belief?

   a.

   b.

   c.

   d.

3. If I were to change my belief to a *positive* one, what would it be?

4. How would the *consequences* be different?

5. What am I willing to change?

5

Making a Plan

Plunging headlong down the freeway at 100-plus miles per hour in a candy-apple red Corvette is my idea of a good time. Ramming through four gears, feeling the mighty surge of automotive power spin the wheels wildly and tilt the front end to meet the challenge would be exhilarating. I've always wanted to be a race-car driver.

Help me live my fantasy. Imagine with me that I have chosen to drive at high speeds, and picture what happens.

I rev the engine to its full capacity, experiencing the propulsion of the car under me. As I pick up speed, I feel adrenaline rush to my brain. I am ecstatic—this is a dream come true!

Suddenly, however, I catch sight of flashing red lights. As I peer into the rear-view mirror, I know that someone wants to have a word with me.

My heart keeps time with the pulsating police-car lights as I nervously edge over to the side of the road and come to a stop. Fumbling through my purse, I find my driver's license.

"Good evening, ma'am," the officer says. "Are

you aware that I clocked you at 106 miles per hour? You are a menace on the highway. Do you realize you could have been killed going at that speed? Not to mention endangering the lives of other motorists. We're here to protect you, but people like you make it pretty hard sometimes. Your license, please."

As I wait, I muse, *Wonder how much this will cost? Probably a bundle.*

He hands me the ticket and I shyly ask, "Officer, do you know about how much this will cost?"

"Well, ma'am, you're getting off easy. Probably only two hundred bucks," he says.

Two hundred dollars! How awful. What a waste. However, I have another option.

Climbing into my red Honda (I can't afford a Corvette), I slap that baby into first gear and *choose* to drive the posted speed limit. Not real exciting.

However, my chances of getting into an accident are greatly lessened. The best part, though, is that I don't have to pay two hundred dollars for a citation. Instead, I can buy something I really want.

Because I choose to discipline myself, no one else has to do it.

Making a decision to live a life of self-discipline sets us *free*. It gets everyone off our backs—parents, teachers, and bosses. What a good feeling.

Conversely, when we choose *not* to discipline ourselves, we can count on there being someone willing to put us in line. And it's usually very distasteful.

Becoming free doesn't just happen. It takes a plan, then it means working the plan.

Getting a Plan

"Hi, Chris. Thanks for coming," I said. "We need to look at your credits for graduation and talk about alternatives."

Chris gulped. I watched his eyes narrow, then squint as he concentrated. His face was ashen. He looked as though he were waiting for the death penalty. He was—at least as far as graduation was concerned. He wasn't going to make it unless he developed a plan and then worked that plan.

We diligently worked out a strategy together.

"Now, Chris," I said, "you will need to take six classes on our campus each semester, plus four more every semester in adult school to graduate. That's twenty classes.

"Unfortunately," I continued, "you've established a pattern of failing courses and cutting school. But if you really want to graduate, Chris, you can. However, it will take an enormous amount of determination and perseverance.

"You're intelligent and there's no reason in the world that you can't do this if you make up your mind," I said. "I believe in you, Chris, and I'm here to encourage you."

Sitting forward, elbows on my desk, brown eyes snapping and a smile beginning to run across his face, he said, "Mrs. Gordon, I'm going to do it. I really am. No matter how many hours I have to spend in school, I'm going to graduate."

A few weeks later, Chris careened around my door and shouted, "Look at this report card, would you? All A's and B's. This has never happened to me before. And I'm already finished with one class in adult school and another one will be done this week."

*   *   *

The setting June sun framed a picture of graduation hats being thrown high into the yellow-blue sky. In the midst of the shouts and rejoicing, I was grabbed and swung around in a bear hug. Chris's face beamed. "I've been accepted at the community college for fall," he whispered.

*   *   *

"Good grief, Chris! How have you been?" I exclaimed. "It's been nearly two years since graduation."

"I've thought of you so many times but just haven't stopped by," Chris said. "I'm doing great at the community college and begin the university in September to get my B.A.—in engineering."

It was another year before he visited again. "Can I bounce a stupid idea off you?" he asked, grinning.

"Sure."

"Remember how I said I'd always dreamed of

graduating from U.S.C.? Would it be dumb to transfer my senior year?"

"Chris," I said, "go for it! You deserve it. You've worked hard to make your goals and dreams come true. I'm proud of you."

*   *   *

Chris graduated (with honors) from U.S.C. while working part-time as a student engineer at a prestigious aerospace company. Upon graduation, he was offered a full-time engineering position.

It's rare to see a person so determined. Most teens would have dropped out of high school, but Chris grabbed onto the plan and worked until he achieved his dream.

Working the Plan

So often grades plummet when parents divorce. That's usually my first clue. And it's understandable. The zest for life is gone and a what's-the-use attitude emerges.

However, it's *vital* to fight the negative feelings. One way to conquer apathy is to have a daily plan.

Goals

- First: Get up on time.
- Second: Arrive at class on time.
- Third: Decide to go to first period, listen in class, and work for fifty minutes.

- Fourth: Decide to go to second period, listen in
class, and work for fifty minutes.
- Fifth: Make this decision every hour for the
remainder of the day.

When you decide to go to each class one by one
(listen and work), you will have one day down—
then a week—soon a month—and finally a semester. Grades will be good and teachers will be off
your back.

A Plan for Home

There's also a plan for home. Here's an idea for a
chart. Pencil in your evening schedule.

	Mon.	Tues.	Wed.	Thurs.
3:00	—Hit the fridge/kick back—			
4:00	Math	Science	Math	Science
5:00	English	History	English	History
6:00	—Dinner—			
7:00	—Do chores and finish homework—			
8:00	T.V.	Phone	T.V.	Fun
		calls		Activity
9:00	—Get everything ready for tomorrow—			
10:00	Goodnight!			

Tips

1. Study the hardest subject first. (You have more
energy earlier.)
2. Do *all* the homework.

3. If you have a project, space it out and do a little each day.
4. College prep courses will take much more study time.
5. Involvement in sports will use most of your free time.

The Payoff

By following a daily schedule, four things will happen:

1. You'll earn good grades.
2. There will be more time to do fun things.
3. Chores will be kept up.
4. Your parents and teachers will get off your back.

The payoff is freedom.

Thinking It Over

1. In what areas do I lack self-discipline?

   a.

   b.

   c.

2. What three things can I *do* to bring about change?

   a.

   b.

   c.

3. Pencil in the homework-plan sheet. Work it for one week. Make changes if needed.

6

Where Are My Parents
When I Need Them?

At my high school, I see lots of broken legs and arms.

Let's say you're the unlucky person and it's your leg that breaks. You are rushed to the doctor. Your leg is set, a cast is put on, and you're out of school for a couple of days. The doctor wants you to rest up because a broken bone is jarring to the body and causes pain.

When you're in pain, you usually think of only one thing—self. You become "me" centered because it hurts so much. You can't cope with your own pain, let alone someone else's. Everything becomes an effort. Ordinary things overwhelm you.

When you get back to school, you hobble around on crutches. Stairs throw you for a loop, so you look for slopes (hopefully the kind for wheelchairs). It's difficult trying to maneuver the crutches, carry books, and get to class reasonably on time. The whole situation is likely to send you into a tizzy.

Meanwhile, you are constantly aware of and protecting the injured leg. When people pass by, you cautiously move the leg out of harm's way. In fact, most of your attention is on the leg, trying to keep it comfortable, unharmed, shielded, and inconspicuous. For about six weeks your main focus is on the injury. During that time you are not capable of taking care of other people. Usually, you don't even notice their needs.

In time, the leg heals and the cast is removed. When the limb is well, you return to being a supportive, caring friend.

Parents in Pain

This is how all of us (including parents) react when separation or divorce hits our lives. Parents are immersed in their pain—absorbed, preoccupied, and engrossed. Their emotional cushion is gone. They don't have a lot of emotional or physical energy to meet the needs of their kids.

"I just can't go on. If it weren't for the kids, well, I'm not sure if I could continue to live," sobbed one separated woman.

Her eyes took on a faraway look. "We met in high school and it was love at first sight. I thought we had a perfect marriage. When I found he was having an affair with my best friend, I wanted to die. I feel like my life's over. My kids will grow up, get married, and leave. And I'll be left alone. Dumped. Forgotten."

Slumped on the sofa, she was the picture of a

beaten woman. Tears cascaded over her cheeks and dripped from her chin. She was so unaware of the tears that she did not even wipe them away.

"Yesterday, my husband called to say I need to get off my butt and find a better paying job, because he isn't going to support me or the kids anymore. I was devastated. I'm desperate. I don't know what to do."

I'm sure you can identify with a lot of these feelings: fear, uncertainty, abandonment, loneliness, hopelessness, defenselessness.

Everyone is in pain.

Striking Out

Sometimes, when we're in pain, we strike out at the people who love us the most.

Sparky is my little, white Highland terrier—a ball of fluff. I couldn't ask for a better dispositioned dog. When I'm gone for a couple of days, she's forgiving and overjoyed to see me when I return. She's never even come close to biting anyone.

However, late one afternoon, I heard her *ki-yiing* in the backyard, which sent me running. She was writhing in obvious pain and bleeding. As I approached her and reached out to try to see what was wrong, she bit me and kept biting me—hard. She drew blood. I managed to get my legs around her in order to hold her while I investigated. I saw that the tie-out chain was wound around her several times and her toenail was caught. It was nearly being pulled out. After a struggle for both of us, I finally got her unhooked and released the nail. Afterward, Sparky kept licking the bites on my hands—as though she were sorry.

Likewise, parents sometimes lash out with biting words because they are in such enormous pain. Often they blame the spouse and take out their frustrations on the kids. They say things like:

"It's obvious I meant nothing to your mom, either. She just couldn't wait to get rid of me. Now she's off on some new toot. She doesn't care for you, either. Just wait and see. Mark my words. Someday you'll see what kind of person she really is."

"You want to know something? We're in this mess because of your no-good dad. He doesn't care about us at all. All he can think about is that whore he's running around with. He wouldn't care if we starved."

Response

It's wise to respond *only* to the pain your parent expressed. Don't get into any of the other stuff. Getting involved in the name-calling and fighting can produce your own fight, and it's unproductive. Here's a better way:

Dad: "It's obvious I meant nothing to your mom, either. She just couldn't wait to get rid of me . . ."

Teen: "Dad, I'm sorry you hurt so much. I know you're devastated over Mom's leaving. At times, I feel overwhelmed with pain, too. I want you to know I love you."

Mom: "You want to know something? We're in this mess because of your no-good dad. He doesn't care about us at all . . ."

Teen: "Mom, I know this is hard for you—being left with all the bills and worries. Sometimes, I'm really scared, too. I'm sorry you're in so much anguish. I love you, Mom."

Responding *only* to your parent's pain is healing—for both of you. In the next chapter, I will deal in depth with how to have good communication skills.

Who's Taking Care of Me?

Parents are *supposed* to take care of their kids. They diapered, fed, dressed, and entertained us as babies. When we were young children, our parents held our hands when we crossed streets, picked us up at school, drove us to ball games, bandaged our cuts, saw that we got our shots and that our teeth were fixed, and protected us. Now that we are teenagers, parents attend our extracurricular involvements, talk to our teachers and counselor, buy school supplies and clothes, set curfew, and get to know our friends. Kids can usually count on their parents.

Enter divorce. Even though your parents are still vitally concerned for you and love you deeply, they are not as emotionally capable of showing their love as they once were. Their separation or divorce sometimes appears to be all-consuming.

Parental attention turns to other things: making a living, clearing out the house and moving, paying bills on one salary, having the use of only one car, living in cramped quarters, trying to deal emotionally with a "third" party.

During these times, you will probably feel as though your emotional needs aren't being met. Perhaps they're not.

Here are a few suggestions to deal better with the situation:

1. Keep telling yourself over and over that both of your parents love you deeply, even though that love may not be expressed for a time.

2. Talk honestly to your parents about your own pain. Say something like, "Sometimes I feel so lonely without Mom living with us. It feels as though my guts have been ripped out. It doesn't seem like the pain will ever go away. The future looks bleak, and I'm scared."

3. Give yourself permission to cry with your parent. Hold onto each other physically and emotionally.

4. Allow your parents to mourn. Give them a little slack.
5. Remember, *this isn't forever*.

In the next chapter, we'll explore more specific ways to deal with your parents. As you practice these healthy principles, your relationship will get better.

Thinking It Over

1. Write a few sentences describing your dad's pain.

2. In a few words, *respond* to his anguish.
   Also, tell him a little about your suffering.

3. Depict your mom's hurt.

4. Write a sentence *responding* to her sorrow.
   Now, let her know your feelings of distress.

7

Getting Parents Off Your Back

Pam's husband went to buy formula for their infant son. He never returned. He was killed in an automobile accident. Pam was left with their son and their three-year-old daughter. As is often the case, several years later Pam remarried. Her second marriage eventually ended in divorce.

In my counseling practice I counsel both widowed and divorced individuals. I have discovered from talking with numerous people that, without exception, both groups feel that experiencing a divorce is far worse than experiencing the death of a spouse. The worst part of divorce is the *rejection*. A mate who once loved you deeply doesn't anymore. Death ends a marriage, but divorce doesn't—the contact continues. It is painful, usually negative, and seems to never end.

Besides the rejection that she experiences, the gut-level truth is that women usually lose out financially when divorce takes place. Divorce does not level the playing field. A divorced woman suddenly can no longer afford to live the same lifestyle. She now has to cope with earning a living and raising children alone, and, more often than not, without any child support. Coupled with emotional rejection and financial instability is the fact that divorcées are often looked on as being some kind of a disease. They're left out. Friends disappear. Gossip is passed from telephone to telephone. They are avoided like a plague. Loneliness prevails. Often the women's hurt turns to explosive rage.

Much of the time, their kids become sitting ducks as the emotional gun discharges Mom's anger. The result is war between parent and child. Let's analyze what happens.

Fact/Feeling Message

Whenever we're hurt and angry, our statements contain both a *fact* and a *feeling* message.

Fact: "Just forget about that new stereo you wanted."

Feeling: "I'm not about to dish out all that money for someone who doesn't appreciate me."

Let's look at the *real* fact and feeling behind this angry statement:

Fact: I'm not going to buy your stereo.

Feeling: I'm hurt because I don't think I matter to you.

The problem is not the stereo purchase. The real

issue is the fear of losing the parent-child relationship.

Generally, we tend to respond *only* to the fact. For instance:

Dad: "Just forget about that new stereo."

Teen: "You just can't let loose of a little money, can you? If it was something *you* wanted, it would be different. You make me sick."

With this response, the teen can count on *never* getting the stereo.

Here's a better way. Respond to the *feeling* message first. The *fact* can be dealt with afterward.

Dad: "I'm not about to dish out all that money for someone who doesn't appreciate me."

Teen: (Responding to his feelings) "Sometimes I come across like I don't care for you. But I really do. You mean a lot to me and I'm grateful you're my dad." (Responding to the fact) "Stereos are pretty expensive and maybe we should just put the idea on hold."

Dad's feelings have not been ignored. He has been listened to. He matters. And maybe now he'll help his teen buy the stereo!

Or, maybe you're like me and have some qualms about your father, because you have been emotionally damaged by him. It's difficult to know how to answer honestly, yet kindly. Here's another suggestion:

Dad: "You can just forget about the stereo."

Teen: (Responding to his feelings) "Dad, I guess I come off as being ungrateful sometimes. I'm sorry." (Responding to the fact) "Stereos are pretty expensive. Maybe we should put the idea on hold."

In answering an emotionally packed message, respond to the *feeling* first, then offer a solution (tell them what you're willing to do).

Here are a few more examples:

Mom: "Money, money, money. That's all you want. I can hardly pay the bills as it is. How can you be so ungrateful? You're getting more like that dad of yours every day."

Teen: (Responding to her feelings) "It's really been hard for you, Mom, since Dad left. I know you're worried about the bills. You've been doing all you can and we kids appreciate it a lot." (Responding to the fact) "I'm going to see if I can get a job to meet my own expenses."

Parents of divorce often put down the former spouse. It's a wise choice to *ignore* the statement about the parent (i.e., "You're getting more like that dad of yours every day") and just respond to your mother's pain.

Mom: "How many times do I have to tell you about the lawn? There you sit watching videos. Our lawn's a disgrace to the neighborhood and you couldn't care less. You know, you're a member of this family, too, and it's about time you helped out."

Teen: (Responding to her feelings) "You're right, Mom. I've kicked back all morning, and I need to pull my weight." (Responding to the fact) "This video will be done in thirty minutes. I'd like to finish it, then I'll do the lawn. In fact, I'll spend extra time and really do a good job for you."

This method can be used not only for parents, but for *all* our interpersonal communication. Here are a couple more examples:

Friend: "Where do you get off telling my secret? I told you in confidence and you blabbed. You can just forget about this friendship."

Teen: (Responding to her feelings) "I can see why you're angry. There was no reason to break your confidence and I'm truly sorry. I was wrong." (Responding to the fact) "Our friendship means a lot to me, and I hope you will give me another chance."

Teacher: "I don't know what to do with you anymore. God knows I've tried. You just won't shut up and work and I've had it. Get out."

Teen: (Responding to her feelings) "Mrs. Long, you've been a good teacher. You have always explained things well and really tried to motivate me. It's my fault." (Responding to the fact) "I'm going to make an effort to listen and work in your class."

Taking Down the Defenses

If you will notice in these illustrations, the teen offered *no defense* when he was blamed. He responded to the feeling message only. He admitted when he was wrong and was willing to be truthful.

By taking down our defenses when we're attacked, the other person is disarmed. *He* now becomes defenseless.

When you're wrong, acknowledge it. Be honest. Your straightforwardness becomes your *defense*.

"I" Versus "You" Statements

Often we get in trouble because we start our sentences with "You . . ."

"You" sounds blaming—usually it is.

● "You make me so mad."

- "You always ..."
- "You never ..."
- "Why don't you ever ..."

Parent: "You're a lazy, disgusting kid! This report card is horrid. You really make me mad. You never do any homework. Night after night you just sit in front of that stupid TV. You're going to be a bum all your life. You disgust me." (Blame, Blame, Blame)

Teen: "Get off my case!"

Parent: "Listen to me, young man ..."

When we hear "you," our hackles go up. We're ready for a fight. As soon as the person breathes, we're in there—defending ourselves. Most of the time, instead of solving the problem, we only succeed in starting World War III.

A better way is to use an "I" statement.

- "I think ..."
- "I feel ..."
- "I believe ..."
- "I would like ..."

The parent needs to talk to the teen about the report card, but he should use an "I statement."

Parent: "Chris, *I* need to talk to you about your report card. These grades are unacceptable. Evidently, homework has not been done. *I* know you're a capable person. *I* want the grades to come up."

Since Chris doesn't feel blamed, he can resolve the issue with his parent.

Teen: "Yeah, Dad, I admit I've been kicking back too much. Count on me to make an effort to raise each of the grades by the next report card."

An opinion is offered. (Chris's dad believed he could do better.) The door is opened for resolution of the problem. (Chris admitted his fault and promised to improve.)

Summary

Getting parents off your back is a viable option, but it takes *practice*.

Remember when you first put on a baseball glove and tried to catch the ball? The glove felt weird. You constantly dropped the ball. But, the more you *practiced* catching, the better you became. Eventually, the glove fit perfectly and the balls slammed into the mitt with effortless ease.

As you consistently *practice* these concepts (responding to the feeling message, and using "I" statements), they will become a natural response. In time, it will feel so normal that you won't have to think about it.

Not only will you get your parents off your back, but your relationship with them will *greatly* improve.

Thinking It Over

1. Think of a situation in which there was a *feeling* and a *fact* message. Write down the sentences.

2. Record your initial response.

3. Think through how you could have responded to the feeling message first, then the fact message. Use "I" statements. Write them out.

4. *Practice* these concepts.

8

Home Sweet Home

October 1 dawned hot. I'd just arrived at work when windows rattled, desks shook, and it seemed like the whole building was about to collapse. My pounding heart felt as though it would leave my body. *Oh, dear*, I thought, *is this the "big one"?* Fear gripped me as I desperately searched my mind for the right action. Looking at the nearly floor-to-ceiling windows in my office, I chose to run for a door jam rather than "drop and cover" under my desk.

We experience many earthquakes in California, and usually I've been at home during them. However, on the few occasions when that hasn't been the case, one thought races through my mind. *Head for home. You've got to get home.*

Home is safe. Most of us have a special feeling about it. When we're sad, terrified, hurt, or sick we want to be home. Sometimes, though, home is awful. Divorce often makes it a place to stay away from. It reminds us of the pain. Even though bad things have happened, home can still be good. It takes time and effort, but we can bring it about. Here are some ideas to make home better.

The Pleasure of a Note

William Shakespeare said long ago, "I'll note you in my book of memory." Notes were meaningful to him and they are meaningful to us. Everyone loves receiving notes. Even preschoolers love to get notes. It doesn't matter that they can't read them. A note is a very special thing—just for them. Teens, too, value notes. They get in trouble for passing notes in class. It's been done for a hundred years, and even today's teens take the chance of being caught because of the value of the message.

We often keep notes—at least for a while. We want a note to be handy so we can read it over and over, especially if it's affirming. Each time we look at it, we feel good.

Even though your home might not be so good, I encourage you to get into the habit of writing notes to other family members. Once you begin, writing notes will become a creative outlet that will not only give you pleasure but will also give the recipient pleasure. Humor adds to the fun of a message. The line "Roses are red, violets are blue" can be a great start to a poem with you making up the last two lines. Or, create your own.

A note can be put on the fridge, placed on a pillow, stuffed in a lunch, stuck on a car windshield, tucked in a briefcase, taped on a mirror, inserted in a brush. Write a note and attach a favorite candy bar, a freshly picked flower, a piece of gum, or any small item that would be a pleasant surprise. Shop for greeting cards the recipient might like. Or write out a joke you've heard. Keep an eye out for comic strips and cartoons.

Note writing is an enjoyable experience that will affect your home life positively. Remember, the feelings connected with notes never go away.

The Warmth of Touch

Touching is vital. Some psychologists say that we need from six to ten hugs a day in order to be emotionally healthy.

An experiment to prove that touch makes a difference in our lives was set up on a college campus. The uninformed participants were a group of college students who had come to the library for information.

Half of the collegians were extended the services of the librarian. She talked to them, answered questions, and helped them find resources. The other half of the group didn't get all that much help. But, they were physically *touched* by the librarian as they left, in a way that seemed accidental.

As each student left the library, a researcher asked if their time in the library had been positive. The results were surprising. The students who had been touched reported a very positive experience. Those who had not been touched (even though they had been helped a great deal) had a more negative response.

Touch *does* make a difference in our lives.

Some people are embarrassed by touch. However, there is a wide range of touching—from a bear hug to a playful jab. It's important to touch and be touched in a way in which we feel comfortable.

"I Love You"

How difficult it is to say these three little words. How much we need to say them as well as hear them.

*   *   *

For as long as he could remember, Larry had always been abused. He kept the awful secret quiet.

"Hi!" he yelled one day as he passed my door.

Something's wrong, I thought. So I called out, "Hi, Larry. Hey, do you have a minute?"

"Sure." He came in and closed my door.

"I get the feeling things aren't going very well for you. Want to talk about it?"

"Oh, it's really nothing," he answered.

Quietly I waited.

"Last night me and my dad got into it," Larry finally said. "He was mad because I didn't do the lawn real good. I didn't edge. So he sorta beat me up."

The sordid tale unraveled. Larry's dad had grabbed Larry's hair, and, holding it, had banged Larry's head numerous times on the bathtub. The blood began to gush. Larry felt weak. His father continued to drag him by the hair all over the bathroom ranting, raving, and cussing all the while. His dad had kicked Larry repeatedly until Larry was gasping for breath.

Larry had been victimized all his life and felt totally helpless to defend himself (the typical response of a victim).

"I thought I was a goner this time," Larry said. "But I should have edged the lawn. I knew better." (Victims tend to defend the abuser.)

"I'm here to protect you, Larry. Count on me to stand by you. However, I'm required by law to file the Suspected Child Abuse Report. Now, here's exactly what will happen ..." I explained the process.

*   *   *

Fortunately, when Larry's parents were contacted by the authorities, they realized their need for professional help and began family therapy.

Several years later, Larry sprinted into my office. *What a good-looking young man he's become*, I thought, *so tall and strong.*

"I have some good news," he announced with

tears welling up in his eyes. "Last night my dad told me he loves me. He's never said it before. It feels so good, Mrs. Gordon. He really loves me."

Too bad Larry had to go through such tough times first. But I was amazed at how meaningful it was for him to hear his father say, "I love you."

Love needs to be spoken.

Most teens and parents have a very difficult time expressing love verbally. Often a note is the easiest way. I encourage you to write one to your parents. Hopefully, they will reciprocate.

The Christmas Angel

Christmas Eve is always celebrated at my house—it's tradition. No one wants it changed.

As each family member arrives, I greet them at the door with a little basket of names. They draw one. Then I give them a pencil and paper. They have just become a Christmas angel. This activity gives everyone the opportunity to love and be loved, to give a note and receive one, and to touch and be touched.

During the evening, each Christmas angel must write a letter of appreciation to the person whose name she's drawn. Then, whenever the Christmas angel chooses, she is to give the note to the appropriate family member.

This tradition has become so special to each of us that we usually save the notes. Often, I've been surprised to read the wonderful things my letter says about me—things that would not have been said in person because of embarrassment. I've read these messages over and over and basked in the sunshine of love.

Both the Christmas angel and the receiver feel love toward one another. It bonds a family together in a way we would seldom take time to do.

Christmas Angel Variation

Another way to do the Christmas Angel is for each member in the home to draw a name two weeks before Christmas.

During those two weeks, the Christmas Angel does nice things for the person whose name he's drawn.

For instance, he sees an unmade bed. So, he makes it and puts a little piece of paper on the pillow that simply says, "From Your Christmas Angel." During these weeks, the Christmas Angel constantly looks for ways in which he can be kind and considerate and leave his "mark."

On Christmas Day, each Christmas Angel is revealed.

Other Ideas

The entire family can be Birthday Angels for a week before the birthday. During this time, the birthday person will feel loved, appreciated, and special as an air of excitement permeates the house.

Drawing names for a Secret Pal is also fun. This can be for a more extended period of time (maybe three months). Rules need to be set. For example:

1. The Secret Pal must be in touch once a week.
2. Little or no money is to be involved.
3. It will go from June 1 through August 31.
4. On August 31 the Secret Pals will be revealed at a family party.

I'm a great believer in little practical jokes. All kinds of funny things can be done on a regular basis. It's critical, however, that no joke is malicious or damaging.

Playing made-up games is also great fun. One time I began a game with the sentence, "I'm grateful for the time I never got caught when I ..."

As each family member finished the sentence and wove his yarn, the tales became wild and crazy. We also learned a lot about each other.

Another time we sat around and told raucous "throw-up" stories. (Our family has strong stomachs).

We once read a long, hilarious Christmas play called, *The Best Christmas Pageant Ever*, by Barbara Robinson. It's a tale about the wild and unruly Herdman family, who hadn't a clue of what the Christmas story was about. They cussed their teachers, talked dirty, hit, lied, and smoked. The whole church was shocked when they wanted to play all the major roles in the Christmas pageant. Their antics make a delightful play.

We passed the book from person to person, and it took all afternoon to read the story aloud. But what a memorable, lively, and amusing time!

Long before Pictionary became a "real" game (manufactured and marketed), we made up our own. Still do.

Summary

These are but a few of the ideas that can help you get started on having an enjoyable home life. Even though there's been intense pain, everyone needs to have fun times. Having fun keeps a family close. When we play together, we are able to be more honest. And when the tough times come, we are more capable of supporting each other.

May yours be a "Home Sweet Home."

Thinking It Over

1. Who needs to get a note from you?

2. Write a few lines.

3. Decide how you will give the note in a unique way. Spell it out.

4. Who needs my touch?

5. Think through how you can touch the person so that you will both be comfortable. Write it down.

6. What fun thing can I get going in my family? List it.

9

Becoming Real—Cut the Phony Stuff

One of my favorite stories is *The Velveteen Rabbit*, by Margery Williams. I'll summarize the story for you.

Once upon a time there was a brand, spanking new velveteen rabbit. It had soft, shiny fur with sparkling bright eyes. The rabbit was the envy of every kid on the block.

His little owner loved Velveteen Rabbit and wasn't happy leaving him on the bedroom shelf to look pretty. No sir. The kid dragged him all over. He slept with Velveteen, cried on him, sneezed and slobbered all over his fur, and just about hugged the stuffing out of him. In fact, after being slept with nightly, carried everywhere, and loved a whole bunch, Velveteen Rabbit began to change.

His stitching came loose. This made his legs wobble funny. Padding oozed out of the worn threads; his scratched eyes drooped and began to dangle over his cheeks.

But the surprising thing was that the *worse* Velveteen *looked*, the less he minded because he was *loved*. Truly loved. He became floppy and strange looking as his little master caressed, petted, hugged, kissed, and adored Velveteen. At the end of the story, Velveteen Rabbit is no longer a stuffed animal. He has become *real*.

When the velveteen rabbit looked good he was not real. When we try to be perfect, have it all together, and look super great—we're just *not real* either. It's only as we stop pretending that we become *real*. And the more real we are, the better chance we have of being *loved*.

Incredible.

Admitting the Truth

For a lot of people, it's pretty hard to admit to a parental separation, especially if their close friends come from two-parent families—ones that look good.

I remember looking out the living room window and seeing my dad's black policeman cap bobbing up and down as he walked toward the back of our house. I was only six years old.

"What's happening?" I asked Mom.

"Daddy's leaving," she replied.

I was too upset to go outside, so I watched everything from the window. Soon, my dad climbed into the car and started the engine. My little brother was halfway in the car, hanging onto Daddy and sobbing, "Don't go. Please don't go." I felt so sad and helpless.

For some reason, I felt ashamed. It seemed that our family was the only one where a divorce had occurred. No one I knew was divorced. For years I pretended that we lived in a nice house, that we had enough money to buy clothes, and that our father still lived with us.

The truth was that Dad was gone, we wore hand-me-down clothes, and we survived on welfare.

Not until high school graduation was I able to tell my closest friend the truth. I had been able to keep the secret because she lived in another town. It took ten years to be honest and stop pretending.

These are my childhood memories. My story.

Admitting Our Pain

Admitting that divorce happens isn't easy. Many young children and teens are in the denial (pretending) stage a long time. In order to become healthy, we need to admit the pain, anger, fear, loneliness, and hate we feel, and acknowledge financial struggles, communication problems, and low self-esteem (to name a few).

Often we act as though nothing is wrong. Everything's okay. Nothing hurts. But it does—a lot. We must acknowledge *pain* to ourselves and to others. There's no way in the world we can have a "normal" life when we've been crushed. Pain has a way of making us feel like we're in a fog. It's very irritating and difficult to understand how people can be so happy when we're feeling desperate and hopeless. Only when we grasp the fact that *pain is an essential part of the healing process*, can we begin to heal.

When close friends ask us how we are, we should tell them rather than deny our feelings. Instead of saying, "Hey, everything's fine. No problem," we should admit, "Right now it really hurts."

When we're willing to admit our pain, two things happen:

1. We get support.
2. We begin to heal.

Admitting Our Anger

Another emotion is *anger*. Some people explode in anger all the time. Others totally deny it. Anger is a normal emotion with which we need to deal.

"I'm really angry this has happened to me and my family. It's so unfair" is a healthy statement. Not only does it admit the truth to others, but to ourselves.

It's vital to have a person (preferably an adult) to whom we can vent our feelings of anger. We need someone to whom we can think aloud, talk it out— someone who will listen without taking offense or lecturing. It helps us deal with anger in a healthy way.

Admitting Our Fear

Fear also raises its awesome head when divorce takes place. We can be overcome by fear, especially at night. All the scary thoughts we've pushed down inside during the day come bursting forth in the dark.

"I'm really scared" is very hard to say. But it's essential. The more we express anxiety, the more it lessens. We're then more capable of dealing with fear rationally.

Admitting Our Loneliness

Admitting that we're *lonely* is also difficult. It's easier to act as though we're doing just fine. But we need to be able to say, "I feel so lonely sometimes. Almost as though I've lost my whole family."

Often each member of the family backs off from the others because he or she is so wrapped up in his or her own pain. We can hardly take care of ourselves, let alone be supportive of our parents and siblings. Yet, as we withdraw, our pain intensifies.

The best thing a family can do is to talk about their feelings together, cry, and hold each other— admitting the intense feelings that have erupted. It will be a relief and will bring the family closer to each other as they walk through the healing process together.

Admitting Our Hatred

Hate can be an all-consuming emotion if we let it. We hate parents, brothers, sisters, friends, employers, teachers—the world. Hate is based on the premise that someone is totally responsible for this horrid divorce and *must* be blamed. If we can't pin it on one person, then we begin to hate everyone and everything—including ourselves. Small doses of hatred are normal. However, hate can grow to gigantic proportions and bring even more disaster.

Sometimes we erroneously believe we could or should have been able to prevent the divorce, and we hate ourselves for not doing so. Nothing could be further from the truth. We're feeding ourselves the biggest lie ever.

Acknowledging Financial Struggles

Admitting to *financial* loss is humiliating. Most families, however, must get used to a lower standard of living after a divorce. Often the family home is sold and mother and children are forced to cram themselves into a small apartment. Money is scarce. There are no more frills—just the necessities. Often, even those are sparse.

It's not easy living at a lower standard. Usually we try to make excuses or lie rather than face the truth. The truth is: "Sorry, my family just can't afford it anymore."

Most of the time, friends understand and won't

press it. If they do, they're probably not what they're cracked up to be.

Acknowledging Communication Problems

Very often, *communication problems* mean there just isn't much communication at all. Everyone shuts up. It's very risky to express grief, so it's easier to stop talking. Each family member is desperately trying to deal with his own issues (or deny them) and doesn't have the emotional stability to "be there" for anyone else.

Talking to an adult friend (youth pastor, coach, teacher, grandparent, neighbor, counselor, or relative) will help you work through the painful process. Because you found a listening ear during the early stages of anguish and learned to become open about your pain, communication with your family will eventually become easier.

Acknowledging Low Self-Esteem

Low self-esteem hits like a ton of bricks when separation or divorce occurs in our lives. It seems like the worse we feel, the lower is our self concept, and we don't have the energy to care. Positive self-esteem is like a foggy dream of the past.

It's okay to feel lousy—for a time. If your self-esteem has not improved in five years, then you're in trouble. But not at first.

As you continue the pathway of emotional

growth, you will eventually feel good about yourself again. In fact, once they complete the healing process, most teenagers view themselves in a more positive light than before the divorce. There's hope.

Repression

It's a beautiful sunny day. Cottonlike clouds are floating in the azure sky. The breeze is gentle and warm. I'm in the deep end of the pool with my enormous, colorful beach ball.

However, I don't want anyone to see the beach ball. For some reason I believe it's *very* important that no one sees it. So I sit on it. Sometimes it wobbles, and I have to keep one hand on it to keep it from rising to the surface.

Even though I wave and say "Hi" to everyone around the pool, my main energy is focused on keeping the ball submerged. When it begins to shift, I get anxious. Since it's vital that the ball stay beneath the surface, it takes a lot of my attention, exertion, and stamina to keep it under water.

Okay, let's say I get sick and tired of trying to keep the ball down and say, "Forget this." I allow the ball to bounce high into the air. Everyone sees the colors and *knows* that I had the beach ball submerged.

Now, I can run around the pool, eat, drink, dive, talk to people, swim, and have fun. I'm free. My energies are released to do whatever I want.

Repressing emotions is much like keeping a huge, brilliantly colored ball under water. Almost your entire strength is narrowly focused on *never letting anyone know your feelings*. Consequently, you have little vitality for anything else.

When we finally decide to let that beach ball pop up (admit to our feelings), we're free—free to work, to love, to enjoy life.

Cutting the phony stuff is how we become *real*.

Thinking It Over

1. Make a statement about your feelings in the area of:

   a. Hurt

   b. Anger

   c. Fear

   d. Hatred

2. What feelings do you tend to repress (pretend they don't exist)?

3. Admit the emotion you fear.

10

The See-Saw Syndrome

Did you ever play on a see-saw on the playground when you were a little kid? I used to love it. However, I was much smaller and lighter than the other children my age. When a heavier child found out that with me on the other end it was all teeter and no totter, most of the time I ended up getting banged in the dirt. Once in a while, though, I would find another kid who was a better match and we could actually go up and down.

*   *   *

"Hey, Gil," I bellowed across campus.

"Yeah, Mrs. Gordon," he responded as he came running toward me.

"I mailed a letter to your house about registration and it came back. Have you moved?" I asked.

"Uh, huh. I'm back at my dad's," he answered.

"Why don't you come to see me tomorrow and we'll talk about this," I suggested.

*   *   *

Gil is one of those students who lives on a see-saw. One day he's at his mom's house and the next at his dad's—or so it seems.

Going back and forth is often based on two things:

1. The parent gets mad and moves him out.
2. The teen gets mad and moves out.

Parental Move

Sometimes it's not the student at all. It's the parent.

Your mom says, "I just don't know what to do with you anymore. You drive me crazy. I can't handle you. You're going to your father's. Let him see how bad it is for a change."

Or your dad says, "Your room's a pigsty. I can't stand this mess any longer. You can just live with your mom. She's as big a slob as you. I've had it."

I've found that the vast majority of teens are super. They want to do what is right, and they want to please their parents. Yet during a divorce, they often become pawns of fighting parents; parents who are unwilling to settle their differences with each other; parents who take out their anger on their children.

So, off the kid goes to his father's (or mother's).

When the newest honeymoon stage is over and things get tough again, he's sent back.

*   *   *

"Julie has been here several times to see you," stated my secretary. "She looks like she really needs to talk. Her eyes were beginning to tear. Poor kid."

Grabbing the phone, I called her teacher. "Could you ask Julie Heddon to see me at the end of the period? Thanks."

Pain was written all over Julie's face. Her eyes were red and puffy. Slumping into the chair, tears began to slip over her cheeks.

"Remember how Dad sent me back to my mom?" she asked. "He flat out told me, 'Hey, I'm sick of all this responsibility. Your mom wanted this divorce, so it's about time she carries the load and sees how much fun it is.' Mrs. Gordon, he already had my stuff packed.

"Well, Mom wasn't too thrilled either," Julie continued. "She's living with this guy, and they don't want me around. Last night I just wanted to sit and watch a little TV with her and eat some popcorn. When I asked if there was any Pepsi left she blew.

"'You think I'm made of money?' she yelled. 'Your dad wants all his privacy and isn't willing to pay any of the bills. I'm sick of him—and you. When you get home from school tomorrow, I'm sending you back to your father. Let him see how expensive you are.'

"Nobody wants me," Julie sobbed.

I knew Julie was desperate. I also knew I had to act. *What am I going to do?* I thought.

"Julie," I began. "Do you have any family near-by—a grandparent, aunt, or uncle?"

"Yeah. My grandma. She's my dad's mom," Julie said. "She really loves me."

I called Grandma Heddon and expressed my concern over Julie's predicament. Then I handed the telephone to Julie, and she sobbed out her story.

"Mrs. Gordon," Mrs. Heddon said, "I've been so worried about Julie. I pray for her every day and I also have a group of my friends praying. I want her to live with me."

Julie's story had a wonderful ending. She went to live with her loving grandparents, graduated from high school, and went to college.

"Ma'am, this plant's for you," stated the delivery man a few years later.

Along with the lovely arrangement, Julie had penned a note of appreciation and gratitude for my help.

Fortunately, few parents are like Julie's. Most parents really want the best for their children and will do everything in their power to bring it about.

The Teen Moves

Sometimes the adolescent wants to live where the rules are "loose." He doesn't like a lot of accountability, and views his parents as demanding when they say such things as: "I don't like these grades. Driving is off limits until there are no D's or F's." Or, "Hey, you missed your curfew by an hour and didn't call. You're grounded Saturday night."

A teenager could respond to one of these scenarios with: "Get off my back! I'm moving to Mom's. I've had it with you and your stupid rules."

And off he goes—for a while.

When things are going well, he stays with the current parent. When things are going badly, he leaves. He may rationalize, "No one has the right to tell me what to do" and becomes unwilling to be accountable to either parent.

How irrational.

This type of thinking sets him up for some hard times. Unfortunately, *all* our lives we will have to explain to someone. Even the president of the United States must answer to other people. Fooling ourselves into thinking we can be totally free is unrealistic and eventually is damaging.

With repeated moves the teen is likely to become emotionally unstable—angry, depressed, sad, and lonely.

Staying Put

Generally, the grass is *not* greener on the other side. It's usually brown.

In some instances, a teen needs to move because

of bad circumstances (e.g., abuse). However, once the move is made, he needs to choose to make the situation work. And to *stay put*.

Gil bounced back and forth between his parents so much it made my head spin—his, too. When he got a better offer, he left. And when things got worse, he moved again. He became more and more discontented and depressed.

After we'd chatted on campus, Gil decided to come to see me the following day.

"Gil," I said, "things are never going to be perfect. Choose which home will be the best and stay there. Don't move again until you're financially on your own."

Wonder of wonders, he took my advice.

During the next year, he began to laugh more, his grades improved enormously, he developed new friendships, and he went out for sports.

"I'm really proud of your progress, Gil," I mentioned at graduation practice. "How did you do it?"

With a twinkle in his eye, he quipped, "Well, you taught me everything I know."

"Come on, Gil," I laughed.

"Really, I just made up my mind to make some of the changes we talked about." He listed:

1. Deciding to stop moving
2. Using the daily chart (homework, chores, TV)
3. Listening to his parents' *feelings* about things
4. Sharing honestly with them

"I would never have believed it, but I'm content and happy, and my life is turning out good," he ended.

Lemonade

There's a saying that goes something like this: "When life hands you lemons, make lemonade." Simple, but insightful.

It means that much of life is under *our direct control*. And, the way we manage life is by our decisions.

Good decisions = Good consequences
Bad decisions = Bad consequences

It sounds almost too easy. But it's true. Our decisions (good or bad) are directly related to the outcomes. *Every single decision* has a *consequence*.

Let's say you get up and take your morning shower but *decide* not to put on deodorant. There are several *consequences*:

1. You will smell.
2. As soon as people get a whiff, they'll take off.
3. Some people will make rude comments.

Since you *chose* (decided) not to use deodorant, you will have to take whatever *consequences* come your way. The truth is, you actually *chose* the *consequences* at the time you made the decision to forego the deodorant.

For the most part, depending on our choices, our lives can be good—or lousy. Take your pick. *However*, there are some events in life (divorce, death, accident, illness) over which we have no control. They just happen. We can do nothing about them.

The good news is: We still have a choice. We can determine how we will *respond* to the event. Our responses govern the end result. You have the power of choice. Use it wisely.

Concentrate on the Positive

In every home, there are positives and negatives. Sometimes adolescents tend to zero in on the negative aspects of their parents' home. What they fail to realize is that no home is perfect. More importantly, however, are the positives. The more we focus on what is beneficial, the better our lives will be.

I encourage you to think through the good things in each parent's home. Write them down.

Decide to fix your attention on, encompass, and aim toward that which is valuable.

Choose optimism, and stop the see-saw syndrome.

Thinking It Over

1. Think through the positive aspects of living at Mom's or Dad's home:

MOM'S

Positive:

a.

b.

c.

d.

e.

DAD'S

Positive:

a.

b.

c.

d.

e.

2. Concentrate on the positive aspects and *decide* to be content, wherever you live.

11

Home Free

It's time to deal with the "F" word.

Forgiveness.

In the last few years psychologists have acknowledged the value that is to be found in forgiveness. It's a favorite topic on TV shows and in books. It's popular.

The concept, though, has been around for over two thousand years. It is God's idea. In fact, forgiveness is not a *suggestion*, it's a *command*—a loving directive from God because he knows it will set us free.

In divorce there's usually a lot of forgiveness to be done. Some things that will need to be forgiven include:

- Parents who couldn't work out their problems
- Infidelity of one or both parents
- Lower standard of living
- Moving to a smaller home or apartment
- Horrendous emotional pain
- Break-up of the family
- Inaccessibility of non-custodial parent

- Parents into their own pain and unavailable
- Embarrassment

Forgiveness is not only for you, but for the relationship you have with your parents. When we are willing to go through the process of forgiveness (the long haul), usually, the relationship with the parent becomes honest, loving, and stronger.

Let's explore the steps that will bring forgiveness.

Admit the Pain

Tom was a senior, captain of the football team, strong, with rippling muscles. He had earned a full scholarship to a Pack Ten university. He was the envy of most seniors because it seemed that he had everything going for him.

Upon walking into my office one day, I was surprised to see Tom sitting in the chair.

"I just can't believe my parents would do such a thing," he said. His shoulders shook as he continued. "It hurts so much. I feel like my guts have been ripped out."

Tom was willing to admit his pain. He was honest about his feelings. He found a safe place (my office) where he could say exactly what he thought.

Find an adult who will listen to you—a teacher, neighbor, grandparent, coach, family member, pastor, or counselor. Express how you feel with a trustworthy adult.

Feel the Anger

Slamming his fist on my desk, Tom said, "It's just so unfair. I hate both of them. They've messed up my life—all of us kids. They just don't give a hang about us. I despise them. I could kill 'em both."

A person can't truly forgive until he has experienced anger. Tom felt secure enough with me to say some violent things. He knew me to be nonjudgmental—one who would listen and not condemn.

Explode, if you must, to your adult friend. Get out the angry feelings; acknowledge the depths of your hurt and hostility.

Confronting the Perpetrator

"Tom," I said several weeks later. "It's important for you to tell each of your parents your true feelings. They need to know your pain and your anger. Do it in a non-blaming way by using 'I' statements. Let's practice. Pretend I'm your dad and confront me."

"Dad," Tom began, "I have to tell you how I feel about this whole thing. I'm so hurt because you've left us. Why you and Mom can't work it out is beyond me. I feel so lonely and depressed—like my life's over. It seems like I've lost you and that's tearing me up. I love you, Dad, but I get so mad, because this just isn't fair to us kids."

Tom was honest about his pain and anger. He

told his dad his feelings—even the bad ones. And by saying "I" instead of "you" it was not a blaming session—just one of truth.

Before you confront your parent, write out a short paragraph (similar to the one above). Then, show it to your adult friend and practice it with him or her a few times. Memorize the main points you want to cover.

The goal in confrontation is to work it out with your parents—to restore the love bond.

Steps of Forgiveness

Forgiveness is a *decision*. (Picture it as the engine of a train.)

Actions are things we *do*, *after* we've made the decision. (Notice how the cars follow the engine.)

Feelings (of forgiveness) will eventually come along, even though it may take a long time. Someday, you will suddenly realize that forgiveness has been accomplished. You will not be able to say exactly when it happened, but you will be certain it has occurred. (Envision forgiveness as being the caboose).

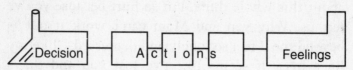

So, what we *do* is vital to the process. Here are some illustrations of actions:

ACTIONS: "Mrs. Gordon," Tom said a few days later. "I talked to my mom and dad—separately. We got our feelings out. We cried. Even though the divorce is still on, I believe we'll be able to continue talking about our feelings to each other. Best of all, I feel I won't lose either my mom or my dad."

Both Tom and his parents were honest with one another. As they expressed their pain, a measure of healing came. They were left with the hope that their talking, bonding, and healing would continue.

ACTIONS: Tom said, "I've decided to spend time with each of my parents and keep them aware of what's happening in my life. I'll do whatever I must to make it work."

Tom made a decision to schedule time for his parents. He was willing to put energy and effort into it. Tom understood that a good alliance would not just happen—he needed to pursue it actively.

ACTIONS: "For now," he concluded, "I've chosen to attend a community college for one year and to let myself heal from the divorce. I also want to be available to my mom and sisters. They need me. I'll put the football scholarship on hold."

Tom chose to take a detour in reaching his ultimate goal. With this plan, he would still be working toward his dream as well as taking the needs of his family into consideration.

Actions are important. What we *do* will greatly determine the outcome of our life.

Forgive and Forget

Some people think we have not truly forgiven until we have forgotten. What a dumb idea! We will *always* remember. An event as excruciating as divorce will not be eliminated from our mind. Over a long period of time, however, some of the more insignificant details will become foggy; but the memory of the event will last a lifetime.

Presently, the divorce is at the forefront, dominating our feelings, thoughts, and actions. Eventually, it will no longer be all-consuming. As each year passes, its influence will become less and less.

Someday, when healing and forgiveness have come, the event of divorce will not have the same degree of significance in our lives. It will not control us, nor will our lives be dominated by it.

That's emotional health.

Giving Up the Right to Retaliate

From time to time, we have a very strong desire to get even for the pain we have had to endure. "I have my rights," you loudly proclaim. "It's unfair. They should pay for what they've done to me."

These feelings are normal. Eventually, though, we must come to terms with forgiveness and give up our so-called right to revenge.

The Hiding Place was a very popular book and was made into a movie a number of years ago. It's the story of the ten Boom family, Corrie, her sister, and her father, who lived in Holland during World War II. They risked their home and their lives in order to hide Jews from Hitler's troops. They were eventually caught and were put into a concentration camp. Corrie was the only survivor.

Following her emancipation, she traveled the world speaking and writing books. I had the pleasure of knowing her.

Sitting by Corrie's bed one spring day, I listened to her stories. I saw the excitement dance across her face as she described the new book she was writing. Her voice was vibrant and alive; her personality, charming. Her whole face beamed with peace, contentment, and love of life.

Corrie had lived through Hitler's inhumanity and the horrors of a concentration camp. Years later, when she came face to face with the Nazi guard who had tortured her, she struggled with whether or not to forgive. She chose to obey her God. She chose forgiveness. And as I looked at the tender, tranquil face of Corrie, I caught a first-hand glimpse of the rewards of forgiveness.

A willingness to forgive is one of the best things we can do for ourselves.

When we forgive, we're home free!

Thinking It Over

Forgiveness cannot be done right away. It takes time—lots of it. It's a process. Even though you may not be able to start on the road to forgiveness now, think it through.

1. To whom are you admitting the pain. Are you really telling it the way it is?

2. Describe your anger. How do you handle the rage?

3. Write down how you can confront your mom.

4. Then write down how you can confront your dad.

5. Whom do you need to forgive?

6. Write down an action plan to begin the process.

12

I'll Take Love Any Way I Can Get It

I've seen that look a thousand times, I thought as Karen stumbled into my office. As she sank into the chair, tears welled up.

"It doesn't seem like things are very good for you today," I said.

She shook her head, and the tears began to cascade down her pretty face. "I'm so scared," she sobbed. "I don't know what to do."

I waited.

She finally blurted out, "I'm pregnant."

Karen's parents had divorced two years earlier. During those dark days, we had spent hours talking about her pain. I sensed her deep desire to be loved and was concerned that she might seek solace by getting involved in a sexual relationship.

It happened. Now the pain was overwhelming.

When parents divorce, there is a great need to *cope.* Some adolescents go for drugs, others grab a bottle, quite a few get involved in sex.

Sure, it's coping—but it's destructive. Actually, it's a cop-out.

Divorce leaves us feeling like our guts have been ripped out. It leaves a big hole that we're *desperate* to fill. Often, we don't think about what the *consequences* of our action will be. We just do it—anything to get relief.

And there is relief, but it's short-lived. Don't mistake relief for a *remedy*. Not only does the relief not last, but sometimes there's a very high price to pay—pregnancy, for instance, or maybe even AIDS.

I believe that one of the reasons it's so common for young people to become sexually involved on the heels of parental divorce is that you *feel* like someone loves you when they pay attention to you. And that's what you're looking for—love.

During the time of separation and divorce, you feel as though your parents don't love you all that much. They're so engulfed in their own pain that you're left to fend for yourself. So you go looking for another love relationship.

"I just want someone to hold me, listen, care, and be there for me" is a statement I often hear. This is a healthy need—but it will *not be satisfied* through sexual encounters.

Seek out an adult with whom you can be honest. Allow tears to come, express your pain, anger, disappointment. Let this person be there for you, to listen to you, to care for you, to encourage you, to pray for you, and to hug you. Use them as your "safe place"—a spot to which you can return as often as you need to.

There are already people in your life who can fill the chasm that is the result of divorce. Perhaps it's an aunt, uncle, grandparent, teacher, coach, neighbor, counselor, youth pastor—someone with whom you already have some sort of relationship. Seek them out. That's constructive coping. It permits healing to occur.

Safe Sex

Television, movies, talk shows, and psychologists have hooked us into believing that sex in an AIDS-filled world is safe. "Just use a condom," they advise.

We feel good when we know things are safe. Statistics say we're safer in a plane than in a car. I've boarded an airplane and flown across the Atlantic Ocean, because I was confident I'd get to the other side. The flight was enjoyable and the food pretty good. During the journey, I watched a movie, read, talked, slept, and played games. Those activities were enjoyable because I felt secure. I've flown over much of the world without mishap. Airplanes are safe, and I feel good about flying.

When teenagers are experiencing the intense pain of their parents' divorce, they want *safety* and *love*. Since the media has *assured* them that condoms are *safe*, some teens choose to engage in "safe sex." They rationalize that they can be loved (through sex), while having a safe, protected experience (through condom use).

However, many other teens don't use condoms at all. Even with widespread information about how deadly AIDS is, and the distribution of condoms, studies show that *few* teenagers use a condom. One student body president said, "Condoms are good and should be used, but when the urge strikes—no one cares." How true.

Thus, *safe sex is a big lie!* Condom, or no condom, "safe sex" is an oxymoron. You are safe from neither pregnancy nor AIDS. A female is able to get pregnant only a few days out of each month. But the reason married couples stopped using condoms years ago is because they *failed*. Medical research states that the AIDS virus may lie dormant for ten to fifteen years prior to a person's becoming HIV positive. A couple is susceptible to AIDS *every day*. That's safe sex? Come on! That's scary. Even if a pregnancy does not occur, a venereal disease is not caught, or the AIDS virus not contracted, a teen is *not left unscathed*.

The hurting teen is searching for love, but when an adolescent becomes promiscuous, the opposite occurs. The emotionally wounded teen will eventually be dumped and will feel sad, lonely, and depressed. Most teenagers wind up feeling used because sex does not fill the deep need to be loved. It seems like such an easy solution, but the aftermath of emotional trauma is deadly.

Instead of dealing with your problems through sex, go to an adult who will take time to listen to your pain. Find someone who will walk with you on the road toward recovery and really care for you. *That's love—and that's safe.*

Staying Out of Bed

"I didn't plan to go that far," I often hear. Many teens do not get into a relationship for sexual reasons. They want friendship and someone who will care deeply for them—to help them fill that void. Yet, most adolescents do not have a plan for staying out of bed. When there's no plan, the chances are great that sexual involvement will eventually happen.

The first step in making a plan is to *decide how far you will go.* For instance, let's say the line you intend to hold is "no sex." Since that is a rather broad parameter you could find yourself involved in a lot of sexual activities—just short of the sex act. Therefore you need to decide *specifically* at what point you will stop. For example, "I will stop at kissing." If you happen to go over the line, you may be disappointed in yourself, but you have stopped short of sexual intercourse.

Dr. James Dobson has given a sexual progression in his book, *Love for a Lifetime.* It can serve as a guideline to help you set your sexual limits.

1. Eye to body
2. Eye to eye
3. Voice to voice
4. Hand to hand
5. Hand to shoulder
6. Hand to waist
7. Face to face
8. Hand to head
9. *Hand to body*
10. *Mouth to breast*
11. *Touching below the waist*
12. *Intercourse*

A brief comment on each category:

Eye to body is noticing another person. Being attracted.

Eye to eye involves both persons seeing each other at the same time.

Voice to voice begins with a short conversation.

Hand to hand involves touching and holding. Mostly nonromantic.

Hand to shoulder is an arm around the shoulder of a friend.

Hand to waist signifies romance is intended.

Face to face is kissing and caressing.

Hand to head becomes more familiar (running fingers through a person's hair). In our culture we do not touch the heads of other people unless we are intimate.

Hand to body is more intimate body examination.

Mouth to breast (self-explanatory)

Touching below the waist is sexual exploration.

Intercourse

At any level, a line can be drawn—one that you decide will not be crossed. The farther a person progresses, the more difficult it is to abstain from intercourse. Dr. Dobson suggests that the last four steps are for marriage. I agree.

A Better Way

Mike, Joe, Chris, and Mark were high-school jocks. Mike was captain of the football team, Joe was a scholar-athlete, Chris earned a full basketball scholarship, and Mark was just a plain, good athlete.

Currently, three of them are finishing their B.A. degrees in college. One has graduated. Even though they're geographically thousands of miles apart, they return home each summer for their annual celebration.

In eighth grade, they made a pact. They decided to remain virgins until they married. This summer marked the eighth year of remaining true to their vow.

That's wonderful.

Over the Edge

Perhaps you're thinking, *Well, it's too late for me.*

The good news is—it isn't. Mistakes can be turned around. We don't need to allow a poor decision to rule the rest of our lives.

*   *   *

I smiled at the lilting voice of Karen. "I had a baby girl last night. She's so pretty. I want you to see her." How different she sounded from the terrified voice I had heard several months earlier.

"I'm waiting for marriage before I have sex again," she told me.

Karen was a wonderful mother during her senior year. She was in the homecoming queen's court and earned a scholarship to a business college.

I truly admire her willingness to admit a mistake, but my greatest joy is seeing her live up to her vow.

It's never too late to *begin again*.

Summary

During the painful time of your parents' separation and divorce, I encourage you to make healthy choices in regard to sexual expression.

Instead of trying to dull your pain with sexual partners, talk to your adult friend. Choose to be sexually responsible.

Go after nonsexual love—it's safe and nondestructive.

Thinking It Over

1. Write the names of adults on whom you can count to listen.

2. Call one of them.

3. Think through your sexual values. Write them down.

4. Look at the events that lead up to sexual involvement. Decide where you will stop.

13

God 'n' Dad: Are They Different?

When our parents divorce, we need God. Even though we also need people, God is the *only one* who really understands the depth of our pain. He knows our helplessness, our anger, our disappointment, our gut-wrenching agony, and our hopelessness. And he cares! We need him in order to get through the divorce.

It wasn't God's choice that our parents divorced. His plan is for marriage to last a lifetime. People are the ones who make the decision to call it quits— not God.

Well, then, why doesn't God do something about it—like stop it? you may be thinking. God allows each of us to make our own decisions about life— good decisions and bad ones. He will not dictate our choices. We have full freedom to select what we will do with our lives. Because of this option, people (such as parents), may make choices that will be painful to us. God will not overrule their right to choose.

God is not unfair. People are.

Differences Between God and Dad

Theologians tell us that we tend to see God the same way we see Dad.

I'm always amazed when I hear a person talking about her father as though he were the greatest thing since sliced bread. Often I've watched how such fathers treat their kids—they show love, concern, affection, honesty. They have fun together. There is trust. I envy that sort of relationship.

As for me—well, I stand around the greeting-card section at the store trying to find *generic* birthday and Father's Day cards. Most of them are filled with accolades to a father who loved deeply, was always there, and could be trusted and counted on. Mine wasn't and so I struggle. I can't bring myself to send a card that is untruthful. It's important to me that I honor my father, but I also want to be honest.

Those of us who have had a father with negative qualities tend to look at God with pessimism.

Views of God

Hopefully, most of you have a father you can trust—one who loves you and is there for you. If so, your picture of God is more likely to be positive. You probably view him as being good, loving, tender, and truthful—one who cares and can be believed.

Others may have a dad who *promises* big—but doesn't come through. He can get you all excited

about an event, but when it approaches he explains
it away—excuse after excuse—and your excitement dies. You've heard it for years. The same old
stuff. When you were a little kid, you really believed
him. Now, you have learned that you cannot put
confidence in his promises. They're a sham.

In your thinking, God is very similar. No way is
he going to bring good things into your life. Sure, he
vows, but you *know* you can't rely on him. So, you
leave him out of your life. Why bother?

Maybe your father is one who is *not there* for you.
When you need him, he's gone. Sometimes he's
physically away, but even when you're in the same
room, he's off in his own little world. He doesn't
want to be bothered. If you try to talk to him about
things that disturb you, he either acts as though it's
not a big deal, or just says, "Uh, huh," as he tunes
you out.

You also tend to see God as being disinterested in
your life. He couldn't care less, you believe. He's
busy doing whatever, and he certainly isn't inter-
ested in your petty little problems. So, why pray?
I'll just have to figure it out myself, you think.

Or, do you have a dad who *demands perfection*?
He's never satisfied. No matter how hard you try,
it's never good enough. You just can't make the
grade with him. He will always point out something
that is wrong, or missing, or not up to his standards.
So, you feel like a failure—at least in your father's
eyes.

How can I be good enough for God? you wonder. You sense God will accept nothing less than that which is flawless. You're beaten before you begin. God will always point out what's wrong, you think. You can't measure up. So you believe it's useless to even try.

As a child, I saw God as a "trick-or-treat" divine being.

We were pre-schoolers. My dad bounced through the door and yelled, "Come on, kids. I brought you some ice cream. Get your spoons and dig in." Out of the paper sack, he pulled a carton. Three wiggling bodies crammed up to the table, and with giggles and dancing eyes, we scooped out the ice cream. The first taste told the sadistic story. It was shortening. Dad shrieked with laughter. "Really gotcha, huh?" he roared. He never produced any ice cream. Our disappointed little faces didn't seem to matter. He was having fun at our expense. It was a cruel joke.

Often in life, I've viewed God as dangling something very desirable in front of me. But, with a quick jerk and lurid smile, he snatches it away, just as I am reaching.

Unfortunately, a few fathers are *abusive*—physically, verbally, emotionally, and/or sexually. Often they are sorry, and the feeling of shame is so intense that tears glisten in their eyes. But they do it again—over and over. The damage is enormous. It has lifelong negative, traumatic effects.

Most abused children and teens believe they are bad persons and deserve the abuse. If you have been abused, you probably feel defeated, a person of little value or worth—an undesirable. Even though you may love your father, you can't trust him. As a victim, you don't feel worthy enough to approach God. You are ineligible for unconditional love. The abuse you suffered, you perhaps believe, is God's fault. So you stay away from the only true source of love—God.

Getting an Accurate View

God is *not* our dad. God is absolute truth—pure, good, just, caring, rewarding, trustworthy, tender— the totality of all admirable qualities.

When you catch yourself equating God with your earthly father, *disconnect*. It's important to stop the irrational thinking and substitute it with reliable reflection. In other words, *tell yourself the truth*. Admit the truth about God. Separate the facts about your dad from the credibility of God.

Over and over I tell myself, "My God is *not* cruel. He does not suspend good things in front of me, then snap them away as my father did. He is *not* my earthly father. God does not trick me. He can be trusted."

I'm finally learning to keep my dad and God separate. I can count on God.

Summary

1. Admit the truth about your father.
2. Tell yourself the *truth* about God.
3. Disconnect from equating God with your dad.
4. Begin to trust God.

Thinking It Over

1. Describe your dad.
   Good Qualities:

   Negative Qualities:

2. How do you see God?
   Good Qualities:

   Negative Qualities:

3. Are there any connections? Write them down.

4. What would you *like* to believe about God?

14

Growing Beyond the Pain

One of my favorite Bible passages illustrates that, no matter how bad things are, God has something better in mind for us:

> "For I know the plans I have for you," declares the LORD, "plans to prosper you and not to harm you, plans to give you hope and a future. Then you will call upon me and come and pray to me, and I will listen to you. You will seek me and find me when you seek me with all your heart. I will be found by you," declares the LORD. (Jeremiah 29:11–14)

Dan

Watching someone throw up makes me nauseous, really sick. I thought I wasn't going to make it when Dan vomited a fifth of vodka into the wastepaper basket in the coach's office. Why they called me, I'll never know.

Trying to keep my eyes away from the sickening scene, I looked at Dan. Long, dirty, greasy hair framed a face that looked much older than his years. His clothes were unkempt and smelly. Alcohol and drugs had already taken their toll on this young man.

I listened to him sob out the gut-ripping account of his parents' divorce. Liquor was the destructive way he chose to cope with the pain.

Four years later, I was heading for the high-school gym when I heard a male voice bellow, "Hey, 'member me?"

Squinting into the bright spring sunlight, I sputtered, "Well, you sure do look familiar."

"Last time you saw me," he said, "I was puking my guts out in Coach Johnson's trash can."

How could I forget!

Dan was one of those kids who, rather than deal with his anger and pain, decided to hit the bottle as well as take drugs. He was unwilling to confront his parents, to honestly tell them of his hurt and anger. He copped out. Alcohol and drugs were the easy road, and he made a deliberate choice to travel down its calamitous, damning path.

"Dan," I said, "how wonderful to see you! What are you doing now?" I could hardly believe it was the same person. He had filled out into a handsome young man, clean cut and almost rosy cheeked.

"I'm studying for the ministry," he answered.

"What?" I gasped.

"Yep. Me and you had some long talks after that experience in the gym—including spiritual ones. I realized my life had to change, regardless of what happened to my parents. I quit booze and doing drugs and made a commitment to Jesus Christ," he said. "I'm in a Christian college and also working with kids as a youth pastor in a small church."

Dan had not only given his life to Jesus, but he had determined a plan of action to rid himself of his addictive behavior. He had signed into a hospital drug-rehab program. It was a tough, painful journey, but he was able to kick the habits. He is currently in a support group for addictive behaviors and continuing to grow.

Occasionally during the next few years I ran into Dan. I marveled at the remarkable change that had come about because of his choice to get treatment and follow Christ.

If you are struggling with alcohol and drugs, it is *imperative* that you get professional help. The telephone book lists such organizations as: Alcoholics Anonymous, AlaTeen, Overcomers, Narcotics Anonymous, and hospital drug treatment programs.

Choose to extinguish your destructive behavior.

Carrie

She was an ordinary looking teen—nothing unusual, a senior.

"Busy?" she asked.

"Never too busy for you, Carrie," I said. "Come on in." One look at her face told me something was terribly wrong.

"My boyfriend's been beating on me. We moved in together a couple a months ago," she added.

Oh no, I thought. *Another abuse case I've got to report to the authorities.*

"Why?" I asked.

"I'm pregnant," she answered. "He's mad and says I have to get an abortion. So I have it set up for Monday. I figure it's the first day of Easter vacation, and it will give me a week to feel good before school begins again."

Tears splashed over her blouse as we talked for the next hour.

So often, adolescents believe that the only solution to their pregnancy dilemma is abortion. They don't have to tell their parents—just quietly get it done. They have been duped into thinking that will take care of everything.

Actually, abortion is an irresponsible, destructive resolution.

Not only do I listen to the enormous guilt and pain expressed by teenagers who have aborted their babies, but my therapy office sometimes overflows with women agonizing over an abortion ten years earlier. The pain goes on.

There is great help and support for those who choose to carry their babies to term. Pregnancy care centers are in every state of the union. They are free. These organizations, staffed with people who care, provide clothes, medical care, and temporary homes. Most large churches can refer you to the clinics.

"I'm not so scared of the abortion," Carrie concluded. "I'm scared of God. Will he ever forgive me?"

Jesus came for just that reason—to forgive. However, we are left to pay the *consequences* of our choices, the effects of which may last a decade.

I thought of her often during the week and prayed.

A different girl bounced into my office the Monday following Easter break.

A brilliant smile danced across her face. She was so lighthearted—no resemblance to the girl of a week ago.

"The most wonderful thing happened," she bubbled.

Yeah, I thought. *An abortion—that's wonderful?*

"Really?" I said.

"Me and my boyfriend went to church Easter," she continued, "and we both gave our lives to Jesus. We couldn't help it—we just had to do it."

"I didn't have the abortion, either," she continued. "We realized we want our baby and really love each other, so we have decided to go back to our parents for now. We're hoping to get married after I graduate."

Not only did Carrie and her boyfriend make the most important decision in life—accepting Christ's forgiveness and turning their lives over to him—but they chose to act responsibly toward their unborn child.

Over the years, I saw baby number one, number two, and number three. Even better, I saw a mixed-up, hurting girl grow into a fine young godly woman because she determined to do what was right.

Summary

Dan and Carrie are success stories for these reasons:

1. They faced their problems head on (parents' divorce, drugs and alcohol, pregnancy).
2. They found an adult who would listen, guide, and care.
3. They chose to cope in a constructive way.
4. They decided on a healthy plan and followed it.
5. They committed their lives to Jesus Christ.

In this book, there are many suggestions on how to survive the divorce of your parents—practical tools that will bring emotional health in all areas of your life.

The first step, however, is giving your life to Jesus. If you need to make this beginning, here is a sample prayer you may use:

Dear Jesus,
   I believe you are God's Son and you came to earth to forgive *my* sins. At this moment, I give you my

life—forgive, guide, and change me. I will do my best to follow you.

                                                        Amen.

Therapy is great, but Jesus is the *answer*.

He will take our painful, messed-up lives and make us into someone beautiful.

Life won't always be easy, but he will be there with us during the tough times—comforting, guiding, strengthening, and forgiving.

"For I know the plans I have for you," declares the LORD, "plans to prosper you and not to harm you, plans to give you hope and a future. Then you will call upon me and come and pray to me, and I will listen to you. You will seek me and find me when you seek me with all your heart. I will be found by you," declares the LORD. (Jeremiah 29:11–14).

Thinking It Over

If you prayed the sample prayer and turned your life over to Jesus Christ, sign this page and date it so you will have a record of this special day.

This is the day I accepted Jesus as my Savior.

_____   _____
Signature   Date

I'd love to hear from you! Please write to me at:

NEW HOPE COUNSELING
908 South Village Oaks Dr.
Suite 250
Covina, CA 91724
818-967-6421